Discover India

by Victoria Marcos

© 2014 by Victoria Marcos
ISBN: 978-1-62395-706-3
eISBN: 978-1-62395-707-0
ePib ISBN: 978-1-62395-708-7
Images licensed from Fotolia.com
All rights reserved.
No portion of this book may be reproduced
without express permission of the publisher.
First Edition
Published in the United States by Xist
Publishing
www.xistpublishing.com
PO Box 61593 Irvine, CA 92602

Banded kraits are venomous snakes that feed mostly on other snakes.

2

Banteng are wild cattle used as working animals. They are also called Bali cattle.

In India, cows roam free in the streets, even in the cities.

It is considered good luck to give a cow a snack.

Bengal tigers are found in various forests and also in the grasslands of India.

They are carnivores that reach 550 pounds and 10 feet in length.

Chital are the most common deer species found in the Indian forests.

Their name means "spotted."

Female chital are much smaller than males and don't have antlers.

Chitals make high-pitched chuckles when they walk.

Clouded leopards have large dark spots that provide excellent camouflage.

They are one of the best climbers in the cat family.

Indian water dragons spend most of their time in trees near the water.

They are excellent swimmers often jumping from branches into the water.

Indian crocodiles are found in freshwater lakes and rivers as well as in the saltwater on the eastern coast.

Indian elephants are very valuable in India.

They are preserved and protected, just as a jewel would be.

They spend up to 19 hours a day eating grass, bark, roots and leaves.

They love bananas, rice and sugar cane.

King cobras prey on other snakes. They are the world's longest snakes reaching almost 19 feet in length.

Ospreys are fish-eating birds of prey.

From the air they can detect fish swimming underwater.

They have a wingspan of almost seven feet.

Peacocks have large tail feathers that are displayed during courtship.

Pythons are not venomous. They squeeze their prey instead of biting them.

Red pandas spend most of their lives in trees. They eat mostly bamboo. They are shy and solitary.

Striped boars are wild boars that are omnivorous.

They are very adaptive to the changing foods that grow in their habitat.

Rhesus macaques live both on the ground and in trees in large groups of 20-200 of both males and females.

Sloth bears noisily suck termites and ants out of their nests. They use their lips like a vacuum.

Tufted gray langurs mostly live in trees in forests.

Unlike other primates, you won't see them around humans very often.

White bengal tigers are rare bengal tigers with white pigmentation instead of orange.

They are a little bigger than bengal tigers.

Sun bears are the smallest members of the bear family.

They have short, coarse fur that helps them avoid overheating and injury from twigs and branches.

Snow leopards are rare animals that live in the mountains of India.

They have powerful legs and can leap up to 50 feet.

Snow leopard cubs are born with a thick coat of fur and are blind and helpless.

www.ingramcontent.com/pod-product-compliance
Lightning Source LLC
LaVergne TN
LVHW021601070426
835507LV00014B/1889